i love beading

i love beading

25 PROJECTS THAT WILL SHOW YOU HOW TO BEAD EASILY AND QUICKLY

JUJU VAIL

PHOTOGRAPHY BY KATE WHITAKER

RODALE

First published in Great Britain in 2009 by
Kyle Cathie Limited, 122 Arlington Road, London NW1 7HP, United Kingdom
general.enquiries@kylecathie.com
www.kylecathie.com

First published in 2009 by Rodale Inc.

Rodale books may be purchased for business or promotional use or for special sales. For information, please write to: Special Markets Department, Rodale, Inc., 733 Third Avenue, New York, NY 10017

Photographs by Kate Whitaker
Illustrations by Harriet Russell
Book design by Kyle Cathie Limited
Printed in Singapore

Library of Congress Cataloging-in-Publication Data is on file with the publisher.

ISBN-13 978–1–60529–931–0 paperback
ISBN-10 1–60529–931–6 paperback

Distributed to the book trade by Macmillan
2 4 6 8 10 9 7 5 3 1 paperback

RODALE
LIVE YOUR WHOLE LIFE™

We inspire and enable people to improve their lives and the world around them
For more of our products visit rodalestore.com or call 800-848-4735

contents

my beading story

I Love Beading – I just don't know what I love most about beading! Is it the delicious fun of choosing those grown-up candies? Or is it the delight of combining different colors and textures? Perhaps it's the pleasure of handcrafting? On the other hand, I also love to own unique accessories and I'm not averse to the compliments I get either. Another thing I like about my beading obsession is that I'm always stocked with special gifts for my female friends. So much to love about beads and beading – why choose one favorite thing?

Like many crafters, I've always had a bead stash. It started small with buttons and some African beads I acquired in fashion design college. Later, I went on to study textile design and my stash grew to include silver-lined seed beads in every color. These I added to my knitting and other fabrics. When I had my children, I wanted design projects that I could make quickly and I turned to my beads. I taught myself bead weaving, stringing and knotting from books, researched suppliers and began to learn about the huge variety of modern and vintage beads available. The stash continued to grow!

I studied cold–connection wire working and lampwork bead making. Pretty soon, I began to experiment with techniques and ideas of my own. I was addicted! I've always enjoyed making what I wear. My interest in beading has married perfectly with my desire to have a unique style that stands out. I customize upscale and second-hand clothing with beads or dress them up with my own accessories. I also make beaded items to decorate my home, which glitter through the dark English winters.

The designs in *I Love Beading* will introduce you to basic beading skills through unique projects. I've designed items with unusual and vintage materials to make them unlike anything you can buy in upscale shops. Plus I've offered many ideas for how you can customize your work to suit your own style.

Whether you're new to beading or already in possession of a sizable stash of your own, *I Love Beading* will be your mantra too!

Juju

beading basics

This section covers the tools, materials, and basic techniques used throughout the book. With minimal investment and just a few skills, many variations of jewelry and decorative items can be made.

tools

The tools and equipment needed for beading are simple, portable, and inexpensive. While some are optional, it is useful to have all of the listed materials on hand to make work easier.

My first recommendation is to get a good set of tools for working with wire and metal findings.

The most essential wire-working tool is a good pair of **needle-nose pliers** ❶. These are my most expensive tool, as I recommend buying the best you can afford. They are necessary for bending wires, working with headpins and other findings. They are also useful for pulling needles through tight spaces and myriad other unexpected jobs. Look for a pair that has a perfect meeting point. The smaller the point, the easier it is to get into difficult places. Look for the same thing in a pair of **round-nose pliers.** ❷

Flat-nose pliers are also essential. Choose a pair that clamp accurately. You may even want two pairs of these for gripping with each hand.

A pair of **flush cutters** ❸ is needed for cutting wire and other metals. I like a pair that meets at a point. Don't spend too much on these, as they wear down after a while and need replacing anyway.

Crimping pliers ❹ are used for closing crimping beads and are also useful for squeezing wire ends into a rounded shape.

Needle files ❺ are useful for filing rough metal edges. Rub the edge of the file over the rough edge of metal the same way you would file your nails, to smooth snags.

The final tool for metalwork is **oxidizing solution** (applied with a **nylon paintbrush**). This is optional but is easy to use and essential if you like the look of 'antiqued' metal.

other equipment

For bead embroidery, stringing and weaving you will need a good pair of **fabric scissors** and a pair of **sharp small scissors** ❶ such as those used for cutting children's fingernails.

Special needles ❷ are used for bead embroidery and weaving in order to fit through tiny seed-bead holes. Beading needles come in a variety of sizes, numbered from 10 to 16. The higher the number, the smaller the needle eye and the smaller the bead size it can fit through. Size 12 sharps are a good all-purpose beading needle, suitable for most seed beads between 10° and 14° in size, and other beads too, including most pearls. Needle size 13 is suitable for seed-bead sizes 10° to 15°, while sizes 15 and 16 can be used on the tiny beads above size 14°. Bear in mind that the higher the needle size, the smaller the needle eye and therefore the more difficult it will be to thread. If you find threading difficult, stick with larger seed beads and needles to begin with.

There are two main kinds of beading needle; '**sharps**,' which are quite short and easy to maneuver, and '**beading needles**,' which are longer. 'Beading' needles are most useful for loom beading and stringing long lengths of beads such as in a fringe. 'Sharps' are a better all-purpose beading needle and most suitable for bead embroidery.

As well as beading needles, you should have **sewing needles**, **tapestry needles**, **pins**, and a **tape measure** on hand to complete the projects.

Special threads ❸ are used for bead weaving and embroidery that are very strong, low twist and easier to thread in small eyes. The most common name for these is the brand name 'Nymo' but there are other brands available too, which are sometimes called nylon beading thread. They come in a small selection of sizes and colors. The most common size is labelled D and is good for most beading with seed beads larger than 14°. When using smaller beads, you may need to work with size O or OO if the D will not fit in your needle eye. Select a neutral shade close to your bead color. Thread can be worked doubled or single depending on the project. The aim is to fill up as much of the bead hole with thread as possible, without making it too difficult to pass the needle through the bead the required number of times.

Clear fishing line ❹ in 10lb and 12lb test weight comes in useful for many beading projects. See page 17 for more information.

Running your threaded needle through **wax** ❺ before beading can prevent difficult knots. After running the thread along wax, run it through your fingers to remove excess wax and straighten any kinks.

Other useful tools to have on hand are **small clamps** ❻ used to prevent beads from falling off incomplete stringing projects; **32-gauge wire** for making beading needles; **white glue, Tacky fabric glue** and **super glue**; an **embroidery hoop** ❼; and **teaspoons** for picking up spare beads.

wire, chain, headpins, and eyes, oh my!

Many of the projects in this book are for jewelry with wire and metal components. A wide variety of metals, in different styles and finishes, is available in shops and from internet suppliers.

Real gold and silver are costly, so better left until you are more experienced. Look for bright and dull gold and silver imitations, as well as a variety of 'antiqued' brass and copper styles. Copper is particularly easy to work with, inexpensive and comes in several finishes.

The projects in this book list the materials they use so that you can buy for each individual project. However, it is a good idea to select one metal style you like and collect a diverse group of components in it so that you will be ready to take on any project at the drop of a hat. That way everything you make will be coordinated.

You will want **headpins** ❶ and **eyepins** ❷ (in a regular and a smaller pearl-sized gauge), **chain** in different sizes and styles ❸, **jump rings** ❹ in at least three sizes (4mm, 6mm, 8mm), a variety of **clasps** ❺ (start with several sizes of **toggle and ring,** and a **lobster clasp**), **earwires** ❻, **connectors** ❼, **charms** ❽, and **wire** ❾ in several gauges (20, 24, 28, 32).

The higher the number of gauge, the finer the wire, so that a 32-gauge wire is as fine as a thread, while a 20-gauge wire is about what you would find in an earwire. You need different sizes for making different components of jewelry.

stringing materials, fabrics, yarns, and ribbons

Stringing materials can make a big design impact in beaded jewelry or they can be nearly invisible.

When you want a stringing material that disappears, try **clear nylon fishing line** (see page 13) or **Fireline beading thread**. These are both invisible and strong and come in a few sizes. Fishing line, suitable for beading with, is labelled 10lb or 12lb test weight. The 10lb test weight is finer and better for using as a bead weaving thread. The 12lb test weight is excellent for stringing heavier beads in a necklace and knots well. Coat each knot in a dab of super glue to ensure they last.

There are a number of cords especially sold for bead stringing. These include **satin cords** in several diameters ❶, **leather** ❷ and **suede cords and tapes**, and **waxed hemp and flax**.

I suggest you think outside the box and experiment with **ribbons** ❸, **yarns** ❹, **embroidery floss** ❺, and **strips of fabric**. Some of my favorite stringing materials are strips of **chiffon** ❻ and recycled **T-shirt jersey** ❼.

seed beads, sequins, and larger beads

Glass seed beads come in a range of sizes denoted by the ° symbol (pronounced 'ought'). Different manufacturers will label their sizes slightly differently, based on length, diameter or hole size, but the numbers give you a rough idea of the bead size. The largest size is a 6°, sometimes called an E bead. These are easy to work with because they have a large hole. There are also 8° and 10° sizes. The most common size is an 11° bead. You will find the largest variety of colors and finishes in this size. Seed-bead sizes continue in 12°, 13°, 14°, 15°, 16°, 18°, 20°, and the ridiculously tiny 22°.

The three main shapes for seed beads are the European doughnut shape, the Japanese tubular shape, and beads with a 'cut' out of one or more sides. They can be used interchangeably but give different results. The cut beads add an extra shimmer because of the faceting.

Some of the more common finishes are matt, opaque, transparent, translucent, iridescent (also known as 'ab' or 'aurora borealis'), galvanized, metallic, silver-lined, white hearts and red hearts. Sometimes these finishes are combined so that you can have a bead that is both matt and iridescent. When bead shopping it is tempting to buy all the sparkly silver-lined ones but they look more interesting combined with opaque or matt beads to set them off.

Sequins come in a variety of colors, sizes, shapes, and finishes. The most common choice is between a cupped shape and a flat shape. The cupped shape will sparkle more. Find a shop that has a large choice of sequins to see the varieties available – it can be hard to judge the finishes on a computer screen.

Beads larger than 6° seed beads are labelled by their diameter or length (depending on their shape) in mm, the smallest of these being about 2mm. Tiny crystals come in several shapes in 3mm, 4mm, and 5mm sizes. These are versatile and sparkly beads. A large variety of beads come in sizes 6mm to 14mm. These are typical 'stringing' beads and are less commonly used for embellishing or embroidering with.

Larger beads come in a huge range of materials: glass, plastic, ceramic, metal, resin, wood, bone, fabric, stone, pearl, minerals, and even feathers. However, when choosing beads for a project, consider the size of the hole as well as the appearance of the bead. It is easiest to work with beads with similar hole sizes within a project. Handmade glass and ceramic beads can have very large holes, while pearls and some stones may have tiny holes. Combining them in a project would take special consideration. Anything with a hole can be used as a bead. Buttons and bits of vintage jewelry make excellent additions, as do homemade elements like yo-yo puffs and tassels.

working with wire and metal

Most of the techniques used in this book are very simple to master, including working with wire and metal. However, I recommend practicing the techniques below before beginning your first project. You need to familiarize yourself with the safety rules and get used to the tool manipulations.

CUTTING WIRE

To cut wire, use a pair of flush cutters. If you look at your cutters carefully, you'll notice that one side is flush and one side has a bevelled edge. The bevelled edge side will create an undesirable point on that side of the wire. You want the smooth, flush side next to the section of wire that will be part of your piece of jewelry.

Place the cutters on the wire with the flush side facing the jewelry piece.

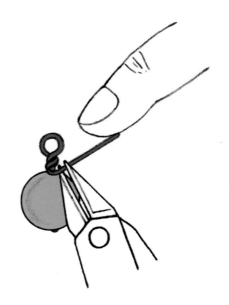

IMPORTANT SAFETY TIP
Place the tip of your finger over the end of the wire. When you cut the wire, your finger will prevent the end from flying away, potentially into your eye.

WRAPPED WIRE LOOPS

This is the way to make a secure wrapped loop at the top of a beaded headpin or eyepin. It is also good for making other kinds of links. For instance, a length of wire can be bent with an eye on either side of a bead to make a unit of chain.

It will usually take a few times to master this, so be patient. Once you've got it, it forms the basis for many pieces of jewelry. You are aiming to get a round loop and a nice tight wrap with the end of the wire around the short stem. Use some inexpensive but easy-to-bend headpins to begin with. Mistakes can be cut free from the headpin with your flush cutters.

ANATOMY OF A WIRE-WRAPPED HEADPIN

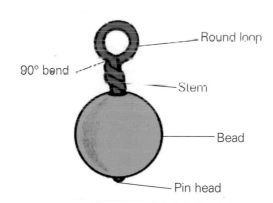

Round loop

90° bend

Stem

Bead

Pin head

WRAPPING THE LOOP

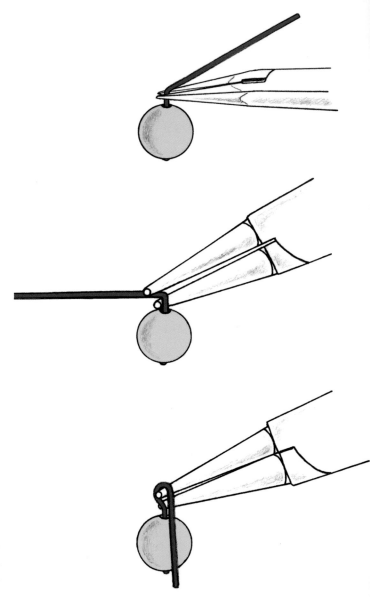

1. Place your bead on your headpin. Clasp the wire as close to the top of the bead as possible, with the tip of your needle-nose pliers. Using your thumb, push the wire over the plier tip so that it forms a right angle facing away from you.

2. Release the headpin from the needle-nose pliers. Switch to a pair of round-nose pliers and use these to grasp the wire just above the bend. The position of the pliers on the wire, farther up or down the jaws, will determine the size of the eye. Using the tip will make a small, neat eye.

3. Using the fingers of your non-pliers hand, push the wire tight around the pliers, towards you, until the wire is facing directly down and facing you. The wire cannot bend any further because it would wrap around the bottom jaw of the pliers.

4. Release your grip on the pliers and rotate them so that the bottom jaw is inside the loop, allowing you to continue bending the wire around the plier jaw until it is facing directly away from you again. Set down your round-nose pliers.

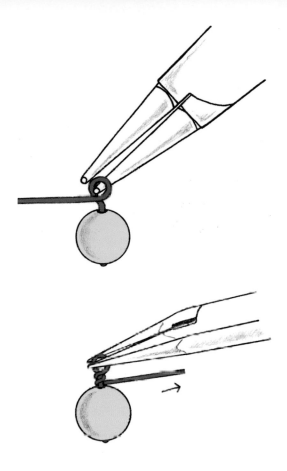

5. Pick up your flat- or needle-nose pliers and grasp the loop sideways, as in the illustration. Use either your fingers or a second pair of flat-nose pliers to wrap the wire around the stem. Pull the wire tightly so that there is no slack between the wire and the stem. The wire should wrap around the stem until it reaches the bead, usually about 2–3 times. You may then wrap the wire back up toward the eye if you have enough wire left and like the look. There are a variety of decorative ways of wrapping the wire, so experiment until you get a design you like.

6. Snip the wire flush with the flush cutters and file the end if necessary.

BEADED HEADPIN ON CHAIN

Place a bead on a headpin and follow the directions for wrapping a wire loop on page 23, until the end of step 3. Slip the headpin wire loop into one of the chain links and continue to wrap the loop with the chain link attached.

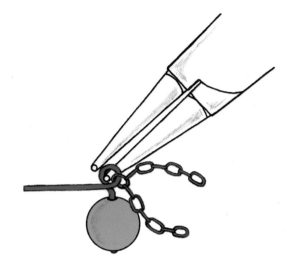

CHAIN JOINS

Beaded chain links can be made using the same wire-wrapping techniques as on the previous page. Different wire gauges are appropriate depending on what you are making. For a strong necklace, it's best to choose a 20-gauge wire, while a delicate pair of earrings may be made with a finer 26-gauge wire.

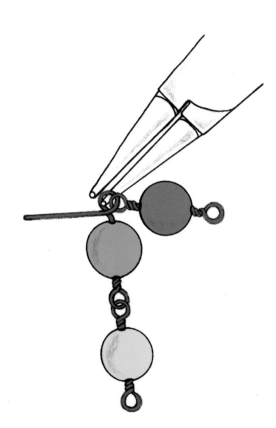

OPENING THE EYE OF AN EYEPIN

To open the eye of an eyepin, grab and pinch the eye with a pair of flat- or needle-nose pliers. Pull the eye toward you to open and back into position to close. Never distort the roundness of the eye shape to open or close it.

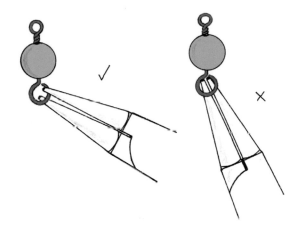

JUMP RINGS

Jump rings are useful for attaching wire and chain elements. They also provide extra articulation, which strengthens jewelry and allows more movement.

A typical use of a jump ring might be to hang several charms from a link in a chain.

It might be possible to hang the three charms directly from the chain link but they would fill up the link hole and hang awkwardly. Hanging them from a jump ring allows for more movement and better structure.

Open and close jump rings with the same method as described for opening and closing the eye in an eyepin. Never distort the round shape! Pull the joining ends to the side to open.

ATTACHING CLOSURES

Most of the closures used in this book are toggle and loop clasps. They come in many styles, sizes, and metals. Keeping an assortment on hand will mean you are always prepared for a beading project.

The trick to making these clasps easy to fasten is to attach a length of chain to the toggle end. This allows the toggle the room that it needs to pivot and slip in and out of the loop. Make a length of chain for the toggle from five linked jump rings.

Other clasp types can easily be substituted in any of the projects. It is recommended that they also be joined with a chain of jump rings in the same manner.

OXIDIZING METAL

I'm a big fan of oxidizing (artificially tarnishing) metal to give it an antique look or just take the brassy shine off a piece. Oxidation works on sterling silver (Bali and Hill Tribe included) and copper, unless the metal has been tarnish-proofed – look out for this when you are buying silver pieces or wire.

I will describe two different oxidizing methods. For either method, work in a well-ventilated area or out-doors.

The simplest method is to buy a blackening or oxidizing liquid such as Platinol. Use a nylon paintbrush to coat the liquid onto the metal. Leave for a few seconds, and then wash the jewelry and brush with water. Buff the metal to a dull shine with a shining cloth. This will make your metal really dark, and the buffing will bring out raised areas of shine.

Another good method is to use eggs. Hard boil about four eggs. Remove them from the water with some tongs while they are still hot. Add them to a lidded container along with your metal to be oxidized. Smash the eggs with their shells still on. Mix the jewelry in with the smashed egg and put the lid on the container. Leave for about 15 minutes, shaking occasionally so that different areas of the metal come into contact with the egg. The sulphur will cause the silver or copper to oxidize. When the process is done, rinse your jewelry well to get all the egg off. You may find an old toothbrush helpful for cleaning. This method will produce a lighter oxidation than the blackening liquid.

stringing and knotting

Knots form a decorative or functional feature in jewelry or bead embroidery.

QUILTER'S KNOT

This is a great all-purpose knot for the end of sewing or embroidery thread.

1. Thread your needle and clip to the desired length. Take your needle with your right hand and the tail end of the thread with your left. Aim your needle and your thread at each other. Bring your hands closer together so that your needle and thread overlap.

2. With your right hand (the one that is holding the needle), pinch the tail of the thread down onto the shaft of the needle. Wind the thread three or four times around the needle. More wraps will create a bigger knot.

3. Without fully releasing your grip on the thread, carefully nudge your fingers onto the coiled thread. Your fingers will stay gripped on these coils until the knot is completed. Release the thread with your left hand and grab the tip of the needle. Pull the needle with your left hand while keeping a good grip on the future knot with your right hand. Pull the needle until the entire length of thread has passed through the knot. A tight tug and you're done! A neat little knot will have formed at the end of the thread.

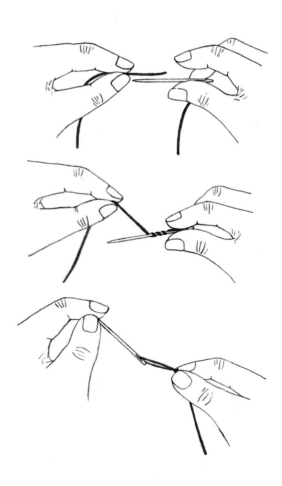

OVERHAND KNOT

I'm sure you're familiar with these. Just bring one cord over and under the other; the same way you begin tying your shoelaces.

In the example on the right the knot is tied with two separate ends. It can also be tied with a single end of cord, as in a traditional pearl necklace.

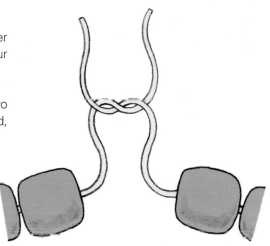

SQUARE KNOT

The square knot is also known as a granny knot or a double overhand knot. It is tied with two ends of cord. Begin by making a simple overhand knot as above by bringing the right-hand cord over and under the left-hand cord. Repeat the process but this time bring the left-hand cord over and under the right one.

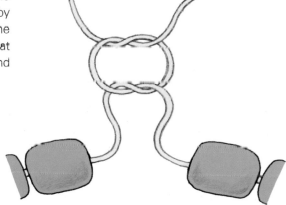

PEARL KNOT

Pearl knots are the small knots in the silk cord between beads on a traditional pearl necklace but can be used with any sort of bead and cord to provide articulation and interest. In this book, frequent use is made of chiffon or fabric strips in place of silk cord.

A pearl knot is made after threading a bead. Make a loose overhand knot. Insert a pin through the knot into the bead hole and tighten, using the pin to ensure the knot lies right next to the bead. With thicker cords, it may not be necessary to use a pin; a fingertip will suffice.

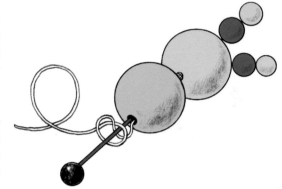

LARK'S HEAD KNOT

A lark's head knot is used to attach the middle of a cord to a connector ring. Fold the cord or ribbon in half. Place the loop made at the halfway point in front of your ring. Take the loop over and in the back of the ring.

Place the two cord ends through the loop from front to back and pull to tighten.

bead weaving

Bead weaving links units of beads with a needle and thread. It can be used to weave flat patterns or three-dimensional objects.

RIGHT-ANGLE WEAVING

Right-angle weaving is a fast way of weaving structures from beads. The beads are set at right angles to one another, forming a slightly open, flexible fabric that reflects light from many angles; perfect for using with crystals and cut beads.

To make right-angle weave, begin with a foundation of four beads joined in a circle. Add three beads in a figure-eight movement. For subsequent rows, first add three beads and then two.

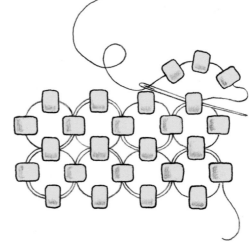

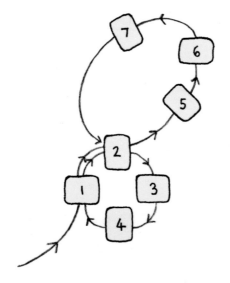

Right-angle weave can also be made up of 'units' of beads larger than four, such as in the example below where each unit is made up of eight beads. In this example beads 1, 3, 5 and 7 will link the units.

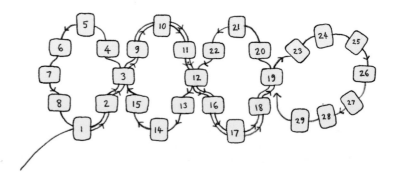

PEYOTE STITCH

Peyote stitch is the most commonly used off-loom bead-weaving stitch. It can be worked in many designs and is ideal for making charted patterns or building 3-D shapes.

Make a foundation row by stringing an even number of beads, twice the number you want in one row (eight in illustration). Pick up a new bead and bring your needle back through the second-to-last bead. Pick up another bead, skip a bead in your foundation row, and go through the next bead. Continue like this to the end of the row. The beads in this row and the previous rows will fall into castellated lines

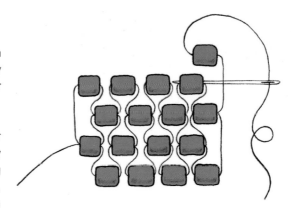

TUBE WEAVING

Either of these bead-weaving techniques can be worked into a tube to make up cords or other shapes with beads.

There are two ways of making a tube: you can work a flat piece of weaving and then link the edges together to make a tube, or you can work in the round as you weave.

It is easiest to work tubular peyote stitch with an odd number of beads in the base row. After you have completed stringing the first row of beads, tie the ends into a circle with a square knot and then continue to add a bead and weave back into the first bead in the first row.

Both stitches can be worked around a mandrel (such as a piece of dowel, a pencil, or knitting needle) to help hold the shape (near right). However, you may find it just as easy to work without one.

A flat rectangle of peyote weaving can also be turned into a tube by weaving the edges together as shown in the three-bead-wide peyote sample (below right).

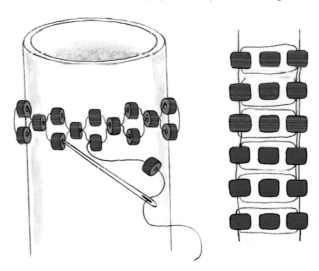

sewing stitches

The projects in this book are designed for hand making; no sewing machine is necessary. However, a basic knowledge of stitching is helpful. The most commonly used stitches are explained here.

RUNNING STITCH

To make a running stitch: fasten a knot at the end of a thread and then bring the needle up and down through the fabric at about $1/8$" intervals.

GATHERING STITCH

Use a strong thread to make a gathering stitch. It is made in the same way as the running stitch but the stitch intervals are longer, about $3/8$" apart. When the gathering row is complete, the needle end of the thread is pulled until the thread gathers the fabric. Make a couple of backstitches to secure the gathering stitches.

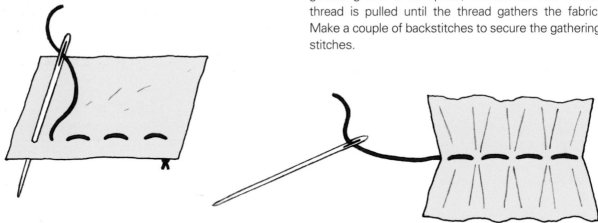

BACKSTITCH

A backstitch is simply a reversed running stitch. At the end of a row of stitching, make a couple of backstitches before tying off the thread with a square knot on the wrong side of the fabric.

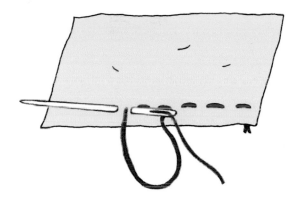

BLIND STITCH (FOR HEM OF SKIRT)

A useful way of hemming clothing. Blind stitch is used to attach the fabric to the skirt on page 111.

Work from right to left with the needle pointing left. Roll the hem edge back about 1/4". Take a very small horizontal stitch in the garment. Take the next stitch in the hem, 1/4" to the left of first stitch. Continue alternating stitches. Be careful to keep the stitches in the garment side very small, and do not pull too tightly. Backstitch after about every 4" to secure your hemming.

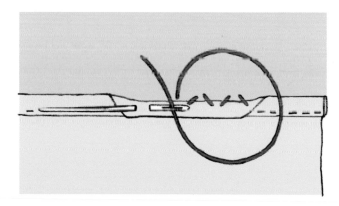

embroidery stitches

Bead embroidery can refer to fabric that is entirely embellished with beads and sequins or it can be a combination of embroidery stitches executed in cotton, silk, or wool mixed with bead embellishment.

WHIP STITCH

This decorative stitch can be used to make a solid line in one or more colors with embroidery threads.

1. Start by making a row of ⅛"-long running stitches. When the row is as long as you want it, tie it off on the wrong side of the fabric. Thread your needle with the same or a different color of thread and poke it up through the fabric next to the first stitch in your running stitch row.

2. Without poking through the fabric, weave the needle from one side of the running stitch to the other. Continue weaving through your running stitches, always sliding your needle under the stitch from the same side. When you come to the end of the row, poke your needle down through the fabric and tie off.

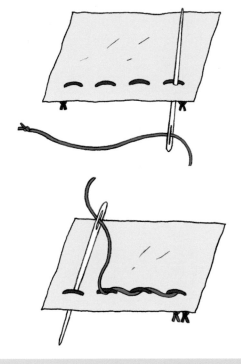

TIP
The thicker the thread and larger the beads, the faster the work is. There is a whole world of exciting embroidery stitches possible, and infinite ways of combining these with beads. To draw embroidery designs on fabric before you begin, use a water-soluble fabric pen or fabric chalk. Some water-soluble fabric pens are set with heat, so remove any trace of it with a spray of water before ironing.

SATIN STITCH

Draw the design on your fabric with water-soluble fabric pen or tailor's chalk. Poke your needle up through the fabric at the lower left-most edge of the shape you're filling in. Make a vertical straight stitch by poking your needle down through the fabric at the top edge of design. Continue to fill the shape with close parallel stitching.

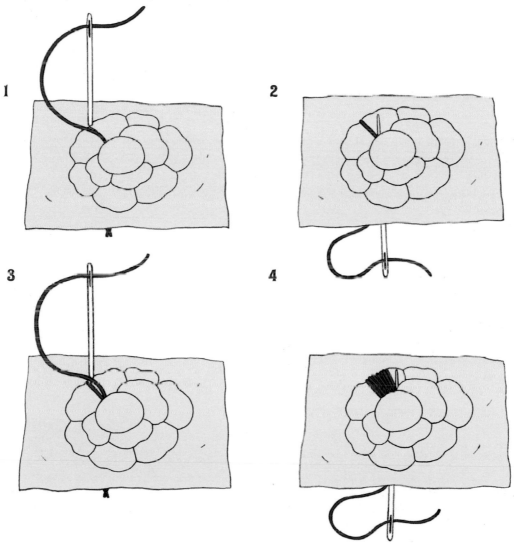

CHAIN STITCH

This is a basic embroidery stitch that can be used for making thick lines or small petal or leaf shapes.

1. Start by pulling your needle up through the fabric until you feel the tug of the knot. With your thumb, hold the thread against the fabric right below where you first came out. Loop your needle and thread around to the right. Keep holding with your thumb and poke the needle in right next to where your thread first came out about 1/8" away. Pull your needle to the left, making sure it travels over the looped thread.

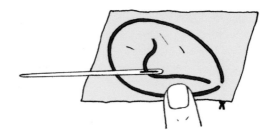

2. Release your thumb and pull the needle all the way to the left. For the next link in your chain, make another loop like you did before. Then poke your needle through, inside your last chain stitch right next to where you last came out, and then out about 1/8" away. Pull the needle all the way to the left again, making sure it goes over the loop thread.

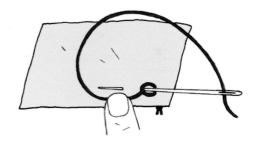

3. Continue by repeating these steps. To finish off or make single chain stitches, poke your needle down through the fabric really close to the left side of your last stitch and pull it all the way through. Knot and tie off the thread.

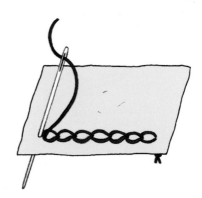

FRENCH KNOTS

A common stitch that looks like a thread bead and is effective when mixed with sparkly seed beads.

1. Start by pulling your needle up through the fabric until you feel the tug of the knot. Hold your needle close to the fabric and, with your other hand, grab the thread about 1" above where it's coming out of the fabric. Wrap the thread three times around the needle, heading towards the tip.

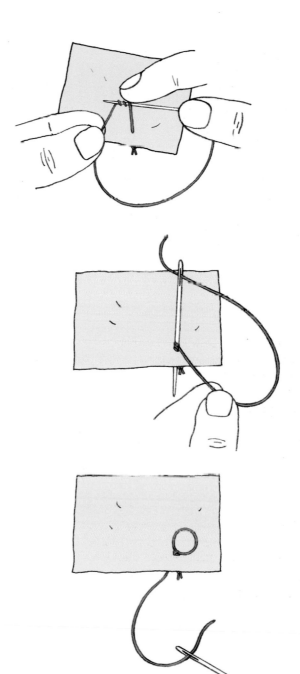

2. Tip your needle while still holding onto the thread. Poke your needle straight down through the fabric extra close to where you first came out. Before pulling the needle all the way through, pull the wrapped thread tight around it. The wrapped thread should slide down against the fabric.

3. Now pull the needle all the way through your French knot until it's snug against the top of the fabric.

bead embroidery stitches

Any embroidery stitch that can be done with yarn or thread can be made to include beads. Many more stitches are unique to bead embroidery.

All the previous stitches can be done with lengths of beads covering the thread. For example, a chain stitch can be made with twelve seed beads in each loop as shown on the right, or a running stitch can be made with three or more beads on each 'run'.

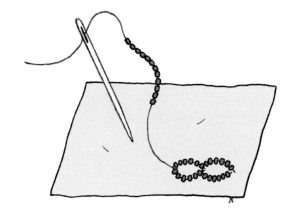

COUCHING

The most common way of attaching seed beads to a fabric is with a couching stitch. Two needles and threads are used for this stitch. One thread is used to string the beads and the second is used to stitch or 'couch' the first in place.

Begin by knotting a stringing thread and bringing the needle up through the fabric. String a sufficient length of beads on the thread. Bring a second knotted thread up where you want the third bead to lie. Bring the needle over the stringing bead and down the other side and pull down through the fabric.

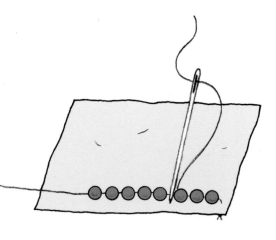

Continue bringing the couching thread up every three beads and couching the stringing bead in place. Manipulate the stringing bead as you go along so that it forms the shape you want your beads to take.

SEQUINS

There are several ways of applying sequins to fabric. Perhaps the easiest is by using a single seed bead to anchor it in place.

Alternatively, a clear nylon beading thread can be used to make invisible stitches. To work a row of multiple sequins, sew a backstitch anchoring the right side of each sequin.

When you get to the end of the row, start a new row of stitching at the right-hand side using backstitch to hold each left side of the sequin in place.

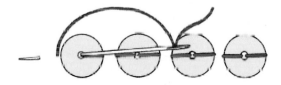

> **TIP**
> **Bead mitt**
> To make bead embroidery faster it is a good idea to stick a piece of double-sided tape to the back of your left (or non-beading) hand. Press the double-sided tape into your seed beads and they will be quick and easy for you to pick up with your beading needle.

To make a row of overlapping sequins follow the sequence of diagrams below.

1

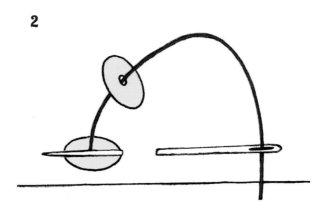

2

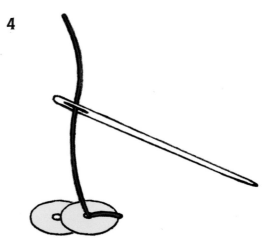

3

4

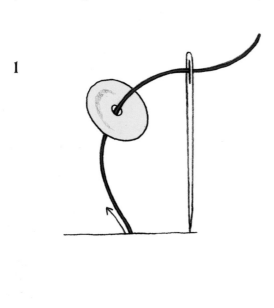

other techniques

MAKING A WIRE BEADING NEEDLE

There are times when you will want to string with a cord that is larger than the eye of any of your needles. To make your own beading needle use a 4" length of 32-gauge wire. Lay your stringing material, about 4" in from the end, in the middle of the wire. Fold the wire in half around the stringing material and twist it.

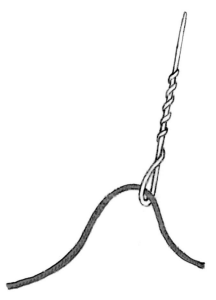

TEARING FABRIC STRIPS

Fabric strips can be used for stringing beads or as other bead embellishments such as the strands of a tassel. Many fabrics will fray if the raw edge is torn and left unfinished. This can be a desirable 'shabby chic' look or it can mean the strip will deteriorate with use, depending on the amount of fray. Test your fabric to see how much it will fray by tearing a strip and then pulling on it and running your fingers along the edge. If it can't stand up to this without fraying, it won't manage longer use. Generally, synthetic materials will fray more than a natural material, which is why I prefer silk chiffon to nylon chiffon for bead stringing and other uses.

To avoid fraying you can cut fabric strips on the bias (45° to the straight of grain) or use non-fraying materials such as leather, faux suede, felt or jersey knits. These will need to be cut into strips instead of torn.

To tear strips of fabric for use, make a small 1 1/8" cut in the selvedge edge of the fabric and then tear across the grain until you get to the other selvedge; cut through it.

YO-YO PUFFS

I love using fabric with beads! It gives me so many more choices and fulfils my craving for pattern and unique colors. These little yo-yo puffs (also known as Suffolk puffs) are great for earrings, brooches or charms on other pieces of jewelry. They can be made tiny, or larger to form posies. Scraps of fabric are all you need. Experiment with small prints and interesting colors. Any kind of fiberfill will suffice for stuffing.

Cut a circle from the piece of fabric. My smallest yo-yos are about 1½" in diameter, whereas a large one for a brooch might be about 4 ¾".

Finger press ¼" of the circle edge to the wrong side of the fabric. Using a strong thread, make a knot in one end and run a gathering stitch around the outside of the yo-yo through both thicknesses of fabric.

Take a small amount of fiberfill stuffing and place it inside the puff. Pull the gathering stitch up around the stuffing and make a few backstitches to hold the gathers in place.

Bring your needle down through the middle of the puff and add a bead, button, tie of ribbon, or a sequin and bead to the center to decorate. Either or both sides of the center can be embellished, depending on how the puff is used.

To make a loop to hang the puff from, use a heavy embroidery thread or cord. Sew a small loop through the edge of the top and then work buttonhole stitch around the outside to finish.

If you wish to hang beads from the bottom of the puff, make another loop in the same way at the bottom.

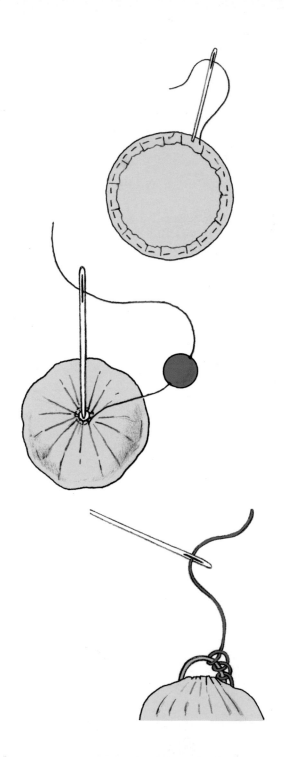

TASSELS

Tassels are easily made out of readily available materials. They can be used to embellish jewelry or home decoration projects. A wide variety of materials can be used to make the strands in tassels. Try knitting yarns, embroidery floss, raffia, strips of fabric, or silk cord. Strands of beads can be mixed in with the lengths of thread to give the tassels extra sparkle.

Decide on the desired length of your tassel and cut a rectangle of strong cardboard of this length by about 4" wide. Wrap your chosen material repeatedly around the length of the cardboard until it looks like it will give a tassel of the required fullness.

Use a tapestry needle to thread a short length of matching yarn under the middle of one side of the cardboard and tie a tight knot around the tassel bunch. Cut the strands of the tassel in the middle of the other side of the cardboard and pull the cardboard away.

Use another length of thread to bind the tassel ⅜" from the top. Wind the thread around all the strands, knotting and weaving the thread end in with the tapestry needle. This can also be done with a length of thread strung with beads so that the tassel is bound at the top with beads.

Trim the tassel ends so that they are even.

necklaces & bracelets

These projects will develop your basic skills while giving you many ideas for endless variations of necklaces and bracelets.

jade elephant

This necklace consists of a simple chain with a linked bead charm. I've chosen a vintage glass elephant dangle to complete mine.

MATERIALS

- 2.5cm jade or other focal bead
- antique copper headpin and eyepins
- 20" antique copper chain (for a short necklace)
- 1 antique copper toggle and loop closure
- 3 antique copper 6mm split jump rings
- 8 x 3mm red glass beads
- 5 x 10mm flat glass flower beads
- 1 antique copper 8mm split jump ring
- glass elephant charm or other charm/dangle

1. Put the focal jade bead on an eyepin and wrap the top loop as shown on page 21.

2. Cut a 1" length of chain and attach to the loop at the bottom of the eyepin. Attach the elephant or other dangle to the bottom of the chain with a 6mm jump ring.

3. Place a red bead and a flower on a headpin and follow the directions for wrapping a wire loop on page 22, up until the end of step 3. Slip the headpin wire into one of the chain links and continue to wrap the loop

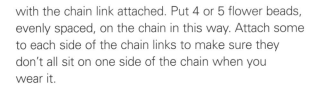

with the chain link attached. Put 4 or 5 flower beads, evenly spaced, on the chain in this way. Attach some to each side of the chain links to make sure they don't all sit on one side of the chain when you wear it.

4. Make another 3 or 4 headpin dangles with just the red bead, attaching them to the chain between the flowers, in the same manner as above.

5. Hold the charm up to your neck in front of a mirror and decide where you want the top of the jade bead to sit. Measure from 3/8" above that point around to the back of your neck. Double this half-neck length to find the total chain length needed and cut the chain to this length.

6. Open the 8mm jump ring and slip it into the top loop of the eyepin holding the jade bead. Close the jump ring and thread onto the necklace chain. Attach a 6mm jump ring to the last link in each end of the chain and attach one part of the loop and toggle closure to each. Close the jump rings and the necklace is complete.

cherry cluster

This enticing pompom of cherry pearls is a versatile necklace. It can be worn extra long, reaching all the way down to the belly button, or shortened by doubling the chain and wearing the pompom at the throat.

MATERIALS

Antiqued copper metal and red pearls were used in this example but you can choose any metal and bead combination.

- 1 yard of chain. Make sure the chain links have enough space to attach headpins through.
- 18 or more 10mm pearls
- 18 or more headpins
- 1 x 8mm split jump ring
- 2 x 6mm split jump rings
- 1 toggle and loop closure (toggle size 2.5cm)

1. Begin by making your charm dangle. Working on an uncut piece of chain, attach as many pearls to each link as possible by following the method for putting a bead on a headpin on page 24. In this example, there are 2 pearls on each link of chain over a 9-link length. It is easier to work with the uncut chain and decide as you work how long and full you want your pompom.

2. When you are happy with the size of your pompom, leave an empty link and then cut the chain above it. The example used is about 1" long. Use the 8mm jump ring to attach the last chain link of the cherry cluster to the ring of the toggle clasp.

3. Use a 6mm jump ring to attach the length of chain to the toggle clasp. The chain in this example is cut after 32". This allows it either to be worn long or for the chain to be doubled through the clasp and worn close to the neck.

Experiment with which length works for you. Use the remaining 6mm jump ring to attach the toggle.

TIPS

This method of hanging beads from headpins off a dangling piece of chain can create a wide variety of focal pieces. The jade elephant necklace in the last project uses the same method but there are fewer beads so the chain is visible. If a chain with larger links is used, more charms can cluster from it and the pompom will be even fuller.

vintage remix

These charming necklaces can be assembled from a collection of vintage beads, chains and costume jewelry, or you can buy new materials and fake the patina with some blackening solution.

MATERIALS

- about 5 x 4mm sterling silver jump rings
- sterling silver loop and toggle clasp
- about 1⅝ yards of 22-gauge half-hard sterling silver wire (it's always good to have a little extra)
- a variety of beads in a limited palette. This necklace used white and blue beads between 4mm and 15mm. Select a variety of shapes and finishes.
- 4" lengths of two or more styles of sterling silver chain. Look for chains with big links.
- sterling silver headpins
- one piece of vintage rhinestone jewelry such as an old shoe buckle

1. Decide how long you want your necklace and then halve this number so that you know when you have reached the mid-way point. Join the 5 jump rings together and link them to the toggle end of the clasp.

2. Cut a 2½" piece of wire and form a wrapped wire loop at one end (see page 22 for instructions). Add a small bead to the wire and then make another wrapped wire loop joining to the last jump ring (follow the instructions for chain joins on page 24).

3. Continue adding beads on wrapped-wire chain joins in this manner until the necklace measures about 4". You can also make rosebuds (see page 76)

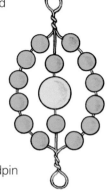

or the following bead wreath and add these instead of a plain bead.
To make a bead wreath, follow the diagram on the right. The spaces between beads in the illustration are for clarity; make yours tighter.

4. When you are making the last wrapped-wire bead chain or charm, attach an 3–4" length of wire to it. Hang a few wrapped-wire headpin charms from the links in the chain.

5. To make the rhinestone charm, clip off any buckle or metal in the back using strong wire cutters and file the cut edges until they are smooth. Use a 12" piece of wire to bend a wrapped chain loop to the chain end. Wrap the remaining end a couple of times around the rhinestone jewelry, exiting toward the center of the buckle.

Keep working with the wire – thread it with beads to fill in the center of the buckle space. Wrap the wire around the other side of the buckle making sure it is balanced. Make a wrapped wire loop to continue the beading and trim any unused wire with your flush cutters.

6. Continue to make wrapped-wire bead chain up the other side for about another 3". Attach a second length of chain to the final bead loop.

7. Hang some more bead charms from the chain links and continue making linked wrapped-wire bead chain until this side is equal to the first. Attach the toggle loop and a charm to the end.

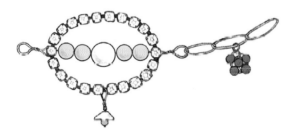

TIPS

Chain is sold by the yard or inch and comes in a wide variety of styles and metals. Sterling silver chain was used in this project but blackened copper would also look nice. Alternatively, use chain from old or broken necklaces. If you plan to patina them, test that they will blacken before you begin. Single rhinestone shoe buckles and dress clips are readily available at flea markets or online auctions. As long as you can wrap wire around them, they can easily be turned into a feature of your jewelry.

long tassel

Sometimes you need a necklace to tickle your tummy button. Wooden beads have a nice earthiness without weighing too much, but you can substitute other styles as long as the 2mm cord will fit through the holes.

MATERIALS

- 5½ yards of 2mm green satin cord. The necklace length will be half the length of the cord used as the knots take up half the length.
- green silk or cotton floss for tassel
- green seed beads for tassel
- 3 x 4mm gold colored beads for beaded ends of tassel
- 120 x 6mm dark wood beads
- 1 x 30mm cloisonné bead for tassel top

1. Begin by preparing the tassel. Make the tassel 4½" long, as described on page 47. The thread used to tie the top of the bundle should be left at least 16" long so that it can be tied into the necklace. After winding the tassel top with the thread, string enough seed beads onto a long thread to wrap around the tassel bundle once. Make a knot so that the seed beads form a tight circle. Bring your

needle through some of the beads and then thread enough seed beads to equal the length of your tassel strands. Thread 1 gold 4mm bead, 1 seed bead and then bring the needle back up though the gold bead and all but the last 2 seed beads in the strand. Add 2 more seed beads and then bring your needle back into the seed-bead ring, 2 beads along. Continue in this manner until you have 3 (or more if you like) strands of equally spaced seed beads. Knot and weave in your thread end.

2. Begin stringing your wooden beads on the cord by making your first pearl knot 4" from one end. String a bead, pushing it next to the knot. Make another pearl knot as close to the bead as you can get. Continue stringing in this way until you have added all your beads.

3. After your final bead, tie the two ends together in an overhand knot. Trim the ends so that they are concealed in the knot. Dot the ends with white glue to stop them from fraying or slipping undone.

4. Thread the tassel tie onto a needle and up through the hole in the cloisonné bead. Bring the needle through a bead knot and back down through the cloisonné bead and top of the tassel. Repeat until the tassel is securely attached. Knot the thread and bury the ends inside the tassel.

TIPS

It is easier to string beads onto a rigid cord. To give the satin cord a rigid end snip the end of the cord at a diagonal and then paint white glue onto 4" of the end. Let the glue dry and then begin beading. As you string the necklace, the glue may soften. Stop and snip a fresh end and repaint the glue to make stringing faster and easier.

chiffon fling

This is my favorite way to string a strand of beads – it can be worn so many ways. The chiffon ties allow the necklace length to be easily adjusted, and the bow can be placed at the front, back, or center of the neckline.

MATERIALS

- 4–12" of silk chiffon in 45 or 60" width, depending on how long you want your necklace
- beading needle wire
- about 20 cream and gold 8mm bicone pressed glass beads
- about 35 yellow 6° beads
- chiffon scrap in contrasting color (optional)
- 2 decorative brass rings
- coordinating embroidery floss

1. Prepare the chiffon by tearing a strip across the width, about ³⁄₄" wide. Trim the selvedge off the threading end and cut at a diagonal angle so that it fits through the bead more easily. Pull off any loose thread ends. Cut lengths of beading needle wire about 4" long. You will probably go through a few of them over the length of the necklace. Twist the wire around the diagonally cut end to make a beading needle.

2. Tie a knot about 4" from the end of the chiffon strip. Thread the first bead on the strip and push it up to the end knot. You may need to use your flat-nose pliers to grab the needle while pulling the bead over the double thickness of chiffon, but after the first one, the beads get easier to thread. Tie another pearl knot after the bead and gently pull on the chiffon

cord. The distance between the knots will grow slightly – that's okay, as it's an opportunity to see more of the fantastic chiffon color.

3. Continue beading in this manner until you have reached a length you like. I beaded for 9" with the pressed glass beads and then finished with 4½" of 6° seed beads with no knots in between. The scrap of pink chiffon is tied in a bow over one of the knots for design interest. Tie a knot after your last bead and leave a 4" tail of chiffon fabric.

4. Attach the chiffon ends to the decorative rings by double knotting around them. Wrap the extra chiffon end around the knot a few times and secure with white glue. Leave to dry. When the knot is dry, wrap embroidery floss around it to conceal the knot and decorate the ends. Use a needle to stitch the floss ends inside the knot and trim.

5. The chiffon lengths that tie the necklace are wider strips of about 1½", 26" lengths of chiffon are doubled for each tie, with the middle being threaded through the decorative ring and tied in a lark's head knot. This means there are 4 ends to be tied into a decorative bow. Alternatively, ribbons could be used – or make several different ties and change them around. The lark's head knots are easy to tie and untie.

TIPS
Before you begin stringing your beads on the chiffon, make some samples to see which width of strip and size of knot works best with your bead hole sizes. I have used ¾"-wide strips of chiffon and knotted them once between the pressed glass beads. If your beads slip over the knot but you can't fit a wider strip through the hole, try making a second knot over the first one to see if this is more secure.

VARIATION
This double-strand variation (right) is only half strung with chiffon knots on the outer strand. After the turquoise bead, the chiffon is tied into a double knot and trimmed. A doubled length of size D Nymo thread is secured into the chiffon knot and then the green sea bamboo is threaded onto the Nymo. This is because the holes in the sea bamboo are too small to fit the chiffon. Bows in two chiffon fabrics are placed over the chiffon/nylon knot to conceal it and decorate the necklace. Where the Nymo meets the glass ring it is knotted and then chiffon fabric and embroidery floss are wrapped over it to match the other side (see below).

string-ball delight

Here's a great way to get a big, light bead in exactly the colors you want by recycling your old T-shirts and using up scraps of thread and yarns.

MATERIALS

- T-shirt jersey or other fabric (see tip)
- assortment of threads, embroidery flosses, ribbons and/or yarns
- about 75 x 4mm fire-polished cut glass beads
- strong beading cord to fit through 4mm beads
- other beads for decoration (optional)

1. Cut your T-shirt (excluding seam allowances and trims) into 1/8" wide strips. Pinch together one end of a strip and start to coil it into a ball. Keep coiling and wrapping tightly into a ball shape by rotating the 'bead' as you wind. When you are happy with the size of the bead, wrap the fabric ball in layers of thread, embroidery floss or yarn for decoration. Allow the layers to peak through, revealing different colors. Finish with a couple of stitches holding the wrapped fibers in place. Continue until you have enough beads to make a necklace. My beads vary in diameter from 1/2" to 1 1/2".

2. Lay the string-ball beads out in a balanced pattern and decide on the length of necklace and how many 4mm beads you want to use as spacers in between.

3. Thread a large-eyed needle with the beading cord and make a knot in the end of the cord. Push the needle through the center of a bead. Use your needle-nose pliers to grasp and pull the tip of the needle as it pokes through the bead. Take a stitch at the end or add a bead (you may need to remove the needle from the cord end in order to thread the bead onto the cord) and then bring the needle and cord back through the bead to the place you started. This first bead will be part of the clasp.

4. Remove the needle from the cord and thread 4mm beads onto the cord. I used 11 beads in this example before I threaded my next string-ball bead.

5. Thread the cord through the needle again and push it through the center of the next string-ball bead.

6. Three 4mm beads follow each string ball until the last one. In this necklace there are 11 string-ball beads in the main body of the necklace, plus one at the end for a closure. After the last string ball is added, string 11 more 4mm beads and then enough 4mm beads to make a loop big enough to fit over the closure bead (25 for my necklace). Double knot the cord around itself at the beginning of the bead loop. Double knot a second time and then put a dab of super glue over the knot. Let it dry and then trim the end of the cord.

crystal link

Chain links are formed here from 3mm glass or crystal beads to make up a versatile necklace. This bead weaving process is known as tubular peyote and can be varied by changing the size or number of beads in the first row.

MATERIALS
- Nymo thread
- each link in the necklace uses 63 x 3mm fire-polished glass beads. There are 9 links, making a total of 567 beads. For a really dazzling (but more expensive) necklace, substitute 3mm round, cut crystals!
- 2 x 3" lengths of ³/₈" black satin ribbon

1. When you have an understanding of the weave structure of peyote stitch it is simple to make tubular shapes. Thread your needle with a single 40" length of Nymo. Pick up 21 beads and fasten them into a circle with a double knot. Leave a 6" thread tail.

2. Pick up a new bead and weave into the second bead in your ring. Pick up a bead, skip a bead on your ring and weave into the next one. Repeat this until you have added 10 beads in this manner. Pick up the 11th bead and weave back into the first bead on this round. You will now be filling in the gaps in this round so that there are 2 beads in each column.

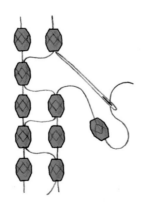

3. Begin the third column by picking up a bead and weaving through the second bead in the last round. Repeat until you have added a total of 11 beads and are ready to fill in the missing beads in the third column.

4. When you have got 3 beads in each column you are ready to weave the edge beads together so that you have a round tube. Bringing your needle and thread up through the right-hand edge bead, pass over the bead in the center column and down through two left-hand edge beads. Pass over the center bead and up through 3 right edge beads. Repeat this stitching pattern until all the edge beads have been sewn together.

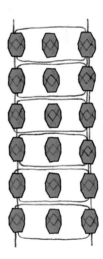

The ring can be made firmer by weaving your thread repeatedly through the beads until the holes are filled with thread. Knot your thread and weave it through a few beads. Trim all thread ends.

5. To make subsequent links join together, you will need to thread the first 21 beads, pass the needle through the last crystal link, and then fasten the thread into a loop before weaving the link.

6. Tidy the ribbon ends by trimming them at an angle. Pass one end of a length of ribbon through the last link in chain and pull through until the two ends are of equal length. Holding both ends together, make an overhand knot near the crystal link. Repeat with the other length of ribbon. Tie in a bow to wear

TIPS

Review the example of peyote stitch on page 33 and make a sample swatch if the technique is new to you. It is very easy to accidentally catch the thread around a bead and create a thread loop when pulling the thread through each bead. Work with lots of light and pull the thread slowly to avoid this. It is useful to wear a bead mitt (see page 41) to make your beads available for easy pick-up.

VARIATION: EARRINGS

Beaded hoops or links can be used as features or components in many pieces of jewelery. These hoops are formed with the same bead-weaving pattern. A pattern of 3 gold and then 3 royal blue Japanese tubular seed beads (Delicas) are used. The larger hoop is made up with an initial ring of 60 beads, using a total of 180 beads. The smaller ring is made with an initial ring of 36 beads, using a total of 108 beads in each hoop. A 1/4-ounce packet of each color is plenty to complete this pair of earrings. Thread the end of the earwire through the bead weaving of a dark section.

zodiac tassel

Look for unusual ethnic trinkets to transform into necklace charms. Here I've used a ceramic Chinese ornament made to celebrate the Year of the Dog.

MATERIALS

- 4" of silk chiffon in 45" width
- beading needle wire
- 36 x 8mm pressed glass beads (mostly green with red used here)
- charm or key ring
- embroidery floss in coordinating colors (yellow and turquoise used here)
- 2 x 10mm antique brass rings
- about 9" antique brass chain
- antique brass ring and toggle and 7 jump rings
- 3 brass heart charms

1. Prepare the chiffon by tearing a strip across the width about ¾" wide. Trim the selvedge off the threading end and cut on a diagonal angle so that it fits through the bead more easily. Cut lengths of beading needle wire about 4" long. You will probably go through a few of them over the length of the necklace. Twist the wire around the diagonally cut end to make a beading needle.

2. Tie a knot about 4" from the other end of the chiffon strip. Thread the first bead on the strip. You may need to use your flat-nose pliers to grab the needle while pulling the bead over the double thickness of chiffon. After the first one, the beads get easier to thread. Tie a pearl knot after the bead and gently pull on the chiffon cord.

3. Continue threading your beads until you get halfway. Add your charm. I have used some embroidery floss to wrap the chiffon where the charm hangs.

4. Continue beading and knotting up the other side until you have two equal lengths of strung beads. Tie a knot after your last bead and leave 4" of chiffon.

5. Attach the chiffon ends to the decorative rings by double knotting them around. Wrap the extra chiffon end around the knot a few times and secure with white glue. Leave to dry. When the knot is dry, wrap embroidery floss around to conceal the knot and decorate the ends. Use a needle to stitch the floss ends inside the knot and trim.

6. Using a jump ring, attach a charm and the length of chain to the decorative ring. At the end of the chain, link together 5 jump rings, ending in the toggle part of the clasp. Add charms to the jump rings if you wish.

7. To the other decorative ring, attach a charm and the ring end of the clasp with a jump ring. The necklace fastens here, rather than at the center back.

The ideal width of the chiffon strip will depend on how big your bead hole is. Start by using a ¾"-wide strip and a fine beading wire. If this doesn't fit through your bead you may need to use a finer wire and/or make your strip a little narrower. You may want to make some tests for the ideal width, before you begin. I loved the look of this dog charm but I didn't like the original tassel colors so I re-threaded my own tassel. See page 47 for instructions on making your own tassels.

TIP
These bangles can be made in
different thicknesses, depending on
how many layers of cord you wrap.
Start by making a bangle with just a
single cord before you experiment
with different sizes. As they get
thicker they will also need to be a
little longer to fit.

bangle wrap

These bangles look great in clusters or mixed in with other bracelets. They are light and comfortable to wear. The instructions that follow are for the top bangle shown in the photograph below.

MATERIALS

- 40" x ½" piping cord
- fine pink cotton knitting yarn or embroidery thread
- about 10 white pearl buttons in different sizes
- red thread
- nude 8mm flower sequins
- purple 8° seed beads

1. My bangles have an interior circumference of 10". Check with a measuring tape that this is a comfortable size to fit over your hand, without falling off too easily. Cut a length of cord measuring 10", or to fit.

2. Grasp your cord firmly, quite close to one end, and wrap the pink thread around the cord, starting at this end. Catch the thread end in the first few wraps. Continue wrapping the cord very firmly (it will compress a little as you go) until you have wrapped most of the cord.

3. Pin and stitch your cord ends together, forming a bangle shape. Wrap more thread over the stitched join until it is covered. This will be slower to wrap since you will have to take the thread in and out of the middle of the bangle.

4. When the bangle is thoroughly wrapped and there is no cord showing, it should be quite firm. If it feels

floppy, continue wrapping the thread on top of the previous wraps until it firms up. Trim the thread with a 8" tail. Thread the end onto a tapestry needle and weave it into the wraps to bury the end.

5. These bangles can be decorated with beads in many ways. This one has a pattern of vintage white pearl beads added with red thread, interspersed with the nude flower sequins and topped with a purple bead.

VARIATIONS

There are so many fun ways to decorate these. Try embellishing them with clusters of chunky coral beads or keep them simple with dashed lines of seed beads.

earrings & rings

These projects work up so quickly that you
can make treasured gifts in an evening.
A girl can never have enough earrings!

rosebud earrings

These rosebuds are made with a simple wire technique, which turns 6 beads into a little rosebud. Large, facetted pearls have been used here but many different shapes and sizes of beads can also be formed into rosebuds.

MATERIALS

- 12" of 22-gauge (or to fit your bead hole) sterling silver wire
- 8 x 8mm faceted bronze pearls
- 4 x 6mm pale gold pearls
- 2 x 10mm blush pearls
- 2 sterling silver headpins
- 2 sterling silver earwires
- blackening solution (optional)

1. Cut a 6" piece of wire and thread 4 of the 8mm faceted pearls onto the middle of the wire. Twist the wires together a couple of times, forming a tight circlet of beads.

2. Make a loop around a pair of round-nose pliers with one of the wire ends. Wrap the wire end around the stem a couple of times as when making a beaded headpin (see page 22). Thread a 6mm pearl onto each of the wire ends.

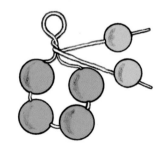

3. Bring the wires down on either side of the circlet so that each 6mm pearl falls to the center of either side of the circlet. Tightly twist the wires together

on the opposite side of the first loop. Make a loop with the round-nose pliers and twist the end around the stem. Trim both wire ends with flush cutters.

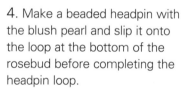

4. Make a beaded headpin with the blush pearl and slip it onto the loop at the bottom of the rosebud before completing the headpin loop.

5. Attach the rosebud and drop to an earwire. Make two earrings the same and then paint blackening solution onto all the wires to make a patina if you wish.

TIPS
Check to make sure the wire fits through all your pearls before beginning. Other beads can be substituted for the pearls, or you may have to change to a finer gauge of wire.

yo-yo earrings

I find so many places to use these little yo-yo puff charms! Follow the instructions on page 44 to make yo-yo puffs in a variety of fabric scraps. Decorate the centers with beads, sequins, nailheads, ribbon, or threads.

MATERIALS

- scraps of vintage silk kimono fabrics
- 8mm orange nailheads for decorating center of yo-yo puffs
- headpins and eyepins to match wire
- 14 pink mother-of-pearl chips
- 4 x 6mm red beads with a white heart
- 24-gauge wire to match earwires
- 2 x 20mm yellow leaf beads
- 2 x 4mm jump rings
- scraps of 1/8" 1/4" wide yellow and pink ribbons
- earwires

1. Begin by making 2 yo-yo puffs as described on page 44 with 1/8"-diameter silk circles. Stitch loops at the tops and bottoms of the puffs and decorate the centers with orange nailheads.

2. Using the eyepins, thread 7 pearl chips and make a wrapped wire loop (see page 22). Trim excess wire. Make 2 of these the same length.

3. Make 4 wrapped wire loop headpins with the red beads.

4. Make a wrapped wire loop in a 4" piece of wire. Trim the wrap end. Add the yellow leaf to the other end of the wire and wrap the wire back up and over

the previous wire wrap at least three times. Trim excess wire. Make 2 of these.

5. Use the jump rings to attach the pearl chip eyepin to the bottom loop of the yo-yo puff. Open the bottom loop in the eyepin and attach one red bead, the yellow leaf and the second red bead. Close the eyepin loop. Do this for both earrings.

6. Tie the ribbons to the jump rings with a bow. In this example there are two ribbons on each earring, one of yellow and one of pink. Dot the tie with a small bit of super glue so that the bow will not come undone. Attach the earwires to the top of each yo-yo puff.

VARIATION
Just the yo-yo puffs with a ribbon rosette and a nailhead bead make a great simple pair of earrings as shown above.

lace earrings

These dangly earrings make a big impact! The surface of the flower is a great place to add sparkle with sequins and beads, while the dangles have lots of flirty movement.

MATERIALS

- lace or embroidered 1" flower and/or leaf motifs
- 2 different kinds or colors of seed beads
- sequins
- beading thread
- 6 x 1/8"–1/4" beads in shades of copper and red
- 4" fine copper or brass chain
- 6 copper headpins
- 3mm copper jump rings
- 5 copper leaf shapes
- copper earwires

1. Begin by preparing your flower motifs. If there are any leaves in your motif, these can also be cut out and used. Embroider both sides of the flower with seed beads and sequins.

2. To make the beaded leaf strand, anchor your thread at one end of the flower before stringing the stems and leaves. I have used a sparkly bronze seed bead for the stem and a matt bead in the same color to make up the 5 beads that form either side of the leaf. Follow the diagram for the thread path. The thread travels down the stem, around each leaf, further down the stem, ending in a leaf, before returning back up through all the stem beads. Make a knot through the flower motif at the top to secure the thread.

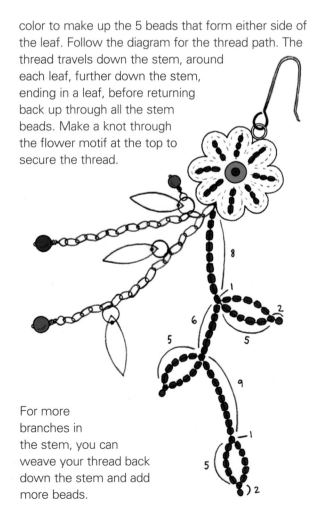

For more branches in the stem, you can weave your thread back down the stem and add more beads.

3. To make the chain dangles, cut the chain into two pieces, each about 2" long. Set aside one chain for the second earring. Select a link slightly off center of the middle of the chain and stitch this to the end of the flower. This will create two strands of chain, one longer than the other. Stitch through the chain link a few times to secure, then knot and trim the thread. Dab a little seam sealant on the thread end.

4. Attach a bead on a headpin to each end of the chain and one near the middle. Use the jump rings to attach the copper (or lace) leaf motifs to the chain at various intervals.

5. Stitch a secure loop or a jump ring at the top end of the flower and attach an earwire.

TIPS

Flower motifs can be bought singly or they can be cut from vintage and new lace trims. To cut them from a piece of lace, use a pair of small scissors to carefully trim off any extra material. After cutting the flower or leaf shapes from the trim, seal the cut edges with fabric sealant or clear nail polish so that threads won't fray or unravel. If you want to stiffen the lace shapes you can paint one side with a 50/50 mix of water and white glue or fabric stiffener.

VARIATIONS
White lace and blue

Lace flowers and leaves were cut from vintage lace and used in these earrings. The lace has been stiffened slightly by painting a fabric stiffener on the wrong side before the motifs were cut out. The leaves were sewn at the end of several of the bead stems. Additional branches with flower and pearl beads were also woven off the stem.

chandelier earrings

Earrings made with a multiple-hole connector are known as chandeliers for obvious reasons. A wide variety of chandelier connectors are available from bead suppliers. This pair includes a place to inset imitation gemstones.

MATERIALS

- 6 imitation gemstones to fit hole on chandelier part
- chandelier connectors
- 10 matching headpins
- 4 x 4mm-round aqua crystals
- 4mm jump rings in matching metal
- 6 x 8mm cut green iridescent beads
- pair of earwires

1. Begin by glueing your gemstones into the chandelier findings. Place a bead of epoxy glue into the stone area, let it settle and level, then use a pair of tweezers to set the stones in the hole. Leave to dry before continuing.

2. For these earrings the tiny crystals on the outer edges needed to be attached with jump rings in order for them to hang properly. Make up 4 wrapped wire headpins with the crystals and then attach with the jump rings. See page 25 for information on working with jump rings.

3. The larger green beads are all attached directly to the chandelier connector. Follow the example of beaded headpin on chain on page 24, substituting the chandelier connector parts for the chain.

4. Open the loop at the bottom of the ear wire (using the same method as opening a jump ring).

Put the top loop of the chandelier on the ear wire loop and close.

VARIATION
These simple chandelier earrings are made with a different connector. A simple red bow at the earwire join dresses them up.

TIPS
You can attach the headpins directly to the
connectors on the chandelier finding or use
jump rings to attach the wrapped loop headpins.
Sometimes the jump rings improve the
articulation of the bead drops. Experiment to see
which works best with your chosen findings.

blossom ring

You can't go wrong with one of these babies on your finger! Nothing sparkles quite like Swarovski crystals, but with only 12 used in the ring, they won't break the bank. These make great gifts if you know the correct ring size.

MATERIALS

- 0.008 (fine) crystal-colored Fireline bead thread or 10lb test weight clear fishing line
- 12 x 4mm bicone Swarovski crystals
- 11° seed beads

1. Cut a 40" length of beading thread and work in the middle so that you have two long ends. Follow the diagram (near right) to make a cluster of 4 right-angle weave crystal units.

2. When you have made the 4 interlocked units, bring one of the thread ends all the way around the outside crystals until it meets the second end. Pull tight and the blossom will cup. Tie with a double knot. The blossom motif is now complete.

You may wish to add a seed bead or crystal to the middle of the blossom – simply weave the thread through to that point, add the bead and weave back out to the other side.

3. Starting with one thread coming out each side, weave the right-angle pattern below with seed beads. Weave circles of beads at each side so that they eventually meet in the middle.

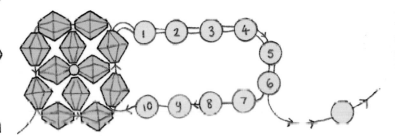

4. How many circuits of right-angle weave you need will depend on your finger and bead size. This ring has a total of 9 but you may need more or less. You may find that after 8 rounds they almost meet and a 9th would make the ring too loose. If this is the case you can make a smaller circle at the back of the ring by adding only 2 beads to the top and bottom of the unit instead of 4.

5. Weave the threads back through the beads until they meet and tie in a double knot. To stabilize the right-angle weave structure you may like to weave back through all the top and bottom beads adding a bead above and below the vertical rungs. Complete the ring by tying the thread end in knots and threading the ends through several beads. Trim thread ends.

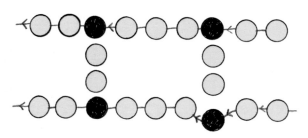

TIP
Familiarize yourself with the directions for right-angle weaving on page 32. If you haven't done it before you may want to make a small sample in seed beads before you begin.

VARIATIONS
The bicone-shaped crystals interlock perfectly to form a blossom shape, however different shapes and sizes of crystal will also work, although the final design may look a little different. Try varying the color of the central 4 crystals to give your blossom a multi-colored effect, or add a 2mm crystal in another color to the center of the flower.

accessories

Don't stop at necklaces, bracelets, earrings and rings; there are so many other possibilities for including beads in your wardrobe. Embellishing fabric with beads adds an extra sparkle to your look.

saucy wrist garter

This stretchy beaded lace cuff slips over your wrist (or thigh) without closures and is very comfortable to wear. You can make it pretty and antique-looking, or bright and garish à la Moulin Rouge.

MATERIALS

- 20" of heavy lace/broderie anglaise trim
- 20" x 1/4"-wide elastic or strips of T-shirt jersey
- 20–30 x 3–4mm or 6° beads. The beads shouldn't be too heavy but the holes should be large enough to accommodate ribbon or chiffon strip. Pearls would be unsuitable because their holes are too small.
- 2 1/4 yards of 1/8"-wide ribbon, or a variety of ribbon and silk scraps. Chiffon strips can be substituted for the ribbon.
- buttons, beads, sequins or trim to embellish cuff (optional)

1. Measure your wrist. The lacy trim should make up a cuff that is at least 1 1/8" longer than your wrist length so it can slip over your hand. The elastic will tighten it to the wrist. Try to find a good place to cut the trim so that the pattern will repeat evenly. Allow a little extra for the lapping of the ends. For my cuff the wrist measurement was 7", the total cuff circumference was 8", and the trim was cut 8 1/4" long so that the ends could overlap by 1/4".

2. Apply Tacky glue to the underside 1/4" of a short edge of the lacy trim. Press the two edges together, overlapping 1/4", with the glued side on top, and leave to dry. When the glue is dry you may add a few stitches to secure.

3. Elastic tightens the cuff to your wrist. Narrow dressmaking elastic, lingerie elastic, stretchy ribbon, and strips of T-shirt jersey can all be used. Cut your stretch strip 2" longer than your wrist length so that you have extra to tie a bow with. Thread the strip in and out of the holes in the trim using the tapestry needle. You can either thread at an edge of the trim, through the center, or in more than one place with multiple strips. When you have completed the entire circumference of the cuff, try it on your wrist to determine how tight your bow should be. Use a pin to mark the spot and then slip the cuff off. Tie a bow in the strip or sew the ends together.

4. Trim an edge of the cuff with bead strands: twist the wire around the ribbon or chiffon strip to make a beading needle. (See page 43 for instructions on making a wire beading needle.) Make a strand the length of the full cuff circumference and join to the beginning with a bow. Don't fill the entire ribbon with beads, leave some space to tie bows along. Use ribbon or chiffon to tie the beaded strand in swags at intervals along the cuff. Dot the bows with fabric glue or a couple of stitches so they do not come undone.

5. Embellish the cuff with beads, buttons, or other trims. I trimmed mine with a row of right-angle weave seed beads.

TIPS FOR SILK CHIFFON

Strips of silk chiffon can be used in place of ribbon for threading beads and making bows. Tear the chiffon into ½"-wide strips and twist the wire into a beading needle near one end. You can use your pliers to help pull the end of the needle through the beads. If the chiffon is too thick to fit through the bead holes, try a ³⁄₈"-wide strip. These strips can also be used for tying pretty frayed bows. If using a thicker silk fabric to make bows, cut the strips on the bias so that they won't fray too much.

TIPS FOR USING T-SHIRT JERSEY

T-shirt jersey can be used to make up the stretch elastic element of the cuff. Prepare the T-shirt by removing all the seams, buttons, trims, and hems so that you have just single-thickness pieces of the fabric left. Cut the T-shirt from the hem to the shoulder in ³⁄₈"-wide strips. These will stretch and curl into tube shapes.

VARIATIONS

White crochet lace (above, middle):
This cuff is made with vintage crochet lace used to trim an old tablecloth. The pink satin ribbon along one edge is lingerie elastic and holds the cuff on the wrist. The wool and bead flower is an appliqué motif that hides the join in the lace.

Peach trim (left):
A fantastic peach colored trim with gold sparkles is used to make this cuff. The sparkles could have been added with seed beads or sequins. Chiffon bows and yellow ribbons tie the bead swags in place.

pretty bow

Bows are back! Okay, maybe they never went away, but decorative, overstated bows are fashionable again. This one is big and beaded. Wear it as a hair clip to dress up long hair or attach a pin and use it as a brooch.

MATERIALS

(All fabric measurements are based on a width of at least 36".)

- 8" piece of dupion silk or other firm-weave fabric
- 8" of stiff interfacing or silk organza
- a group of beads and sequins in different shapes and finishes in a limited palette. The beads used in this project were:

  sequins: 8mm beige flower, 10mm transparent opalescent yellow cup, 4mm pale pink opalescent cup

  seed beads: pale pink opalescent, transparent opalescent white, opaque white

  other: 3mm plastic pearls, bronze 8° Hex, 3mm brushed gold bugles

- 4" long hair clip or brooch back
- beading thread
- 8" of contrasting fabric

1. Mark a 16" x 4" rectangle on the silk fabric using a chalk pencil. Fuse the interfacing or baste the organza to the wrong side of the fabric. Along the 16" length, mark four lines, 4" apart. The center line will be the middle of the bow, while the two squares on either side will form the areas for beading. Do not embroider anything within the center 2". Do all the bead embroidery before cutting the fabric out since it is easier to hoop like this.

2. Put one of the beading squares in the center of an embroidery hoop. Follow the diagram on page 99 for beading using the beads and sequins to embroider the pattern on either side of the bow.

3. Draw a 3/8" seam allowance around the marked rectangle and cut out the fabric. Lay the rectangle on top of the contrasting fabric and cut out a second piece the same size. Stitch the long ends of the embroidered fabric to the long ends of the contrasting fabric with the rights sides facing each other (the embroidery will be on the inside). Turn the rectangle right side out.

4. Fold the bow so the short ends meet and finger press the seam allowances for the short sides to the inside of the bow. Blind stitch the short ends together with the seam allowances tucked into the inside.

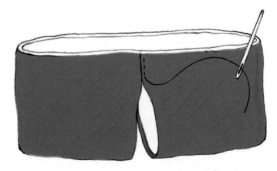

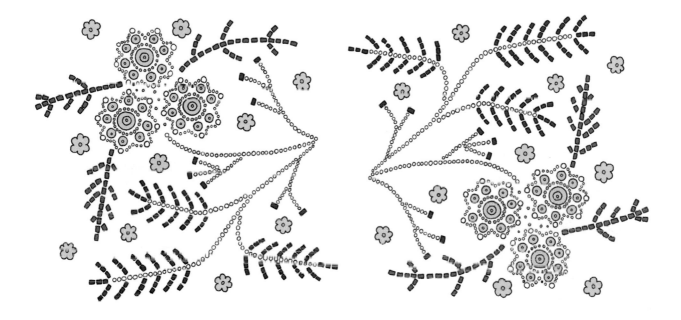

5. Give the bow shape by gather stitching across the middle through all the layers and pulling the bow into shape. Tack the gathers in place. Cut a strip of contrasting fabric, 2" x 4¾" long. Fold the edge of the long ends of the strip to the wrong side to create neat edges. Wrap and pin this strip around the bow to create the centerpiece. Stitch the strip in place and neaten the underside by tucking the raw edges of the fabric to the wrong side. You may wish to make some tucks in the centerpiece or add some more beading to it.

6. Sew a large hair clip or brooch back to the wrong side of the bow.

TIPS

Decorative bows always look deceptively simple but they are rarely tied in place. Most accessory bows are sewn to create just the right shape. You may find that it takes a little bit of fiddling with the central tucks and gathers to get your bow looking just perfect. Take your time and hold it back to evaluate the look.

vintage hairband

This charming hairband is made from a lucky dip into a vintage button box. I've stuck to a color theme of blue, green, and white.

MATERIALS

- at least 8 x ½"–1¼" buttons. You may wish to stack small buttons on top of larger ones to decorate the center, in which case you will need more than 8, and beads, buttons, and sequins for decorating button centers
- 10lb test weight fishing line or fine Fireline beading thread
- 11° turquoise and 8° blue seed beads
- needle and thread to match ribbon color
- 16" elastic ribbon

1. Gather your buttons together and experiment with how you want to compose them. Also experiment with stacking buttons with holes.

2. Cut a 40" length of fishing line or Fireline beading thread. Thread 5 turquoise, 1 blue and another 5 turquoise seed beads to the center of the beading thread. Thread both ends through opposite sides of a blue bead. You've created an end loop, which will be used to attach the elastic ribbon.

3. Begin threading in a right-angle weave pattern following the diagram below.

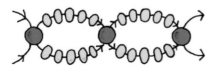

Add a button after every 2 or 3 blue beads in the pattern – if leaving only 2 blue beads between the buttons means they will overlap, you need to weave another circle in the pattern. You are aiming to have all the spaces between buttons look about equal. If you are adding a button with a shank, thread through the shank from opposite directions.

If you are adding a button with holes, don't add the blue bead. After the turquoise beads, thread each end up a buttonhole then work both ends together through smaller button, sequins or the bead on top. Separate the ends to bring them each down a separate buttonhole. Continue beading pattern.

4. When you have added all 8 buttons, weave 2 more circles in the pattern and then bring the ends back through the turquoise beads. When they meet back at the next blue bead, tie a double knot in them. Weave them through some more beads and tie another knot; repeat a couple more times. Finally trim the thread ends and seal the knots with super glue.

5. Decide on the length of ribbon needed to make a snug headband. Hem each end of the ribbon, wrapping it around the final loops.

puff pincushion

Having a pincushion on your wrist is handy for sewing and embroidery – why not embellish it with beads?

MATERIALS
- scrap fabric for puff
- fibrefill stuffing
- embroidery floss
- beads
- scrap fabric for band
- sew-on snap fasteners, size 4

1. Cut a fabric circle 6" in diameter for your puff. Follow the directions for making a yo-yo puff on page 44 up until stuffing.

2. Stuff with a large wad of fiberfill. This will be firmer and fuller than a normal yo-yo puff. Pull the gathering stitches closed and make a couple of backstitches.

3. Thread your needle with embroidery floss and make a knot. Bring the needle up from the gathered side of the puff to the center of the opposite side. Tack in place a few times so that the puff dents in the middle. Now make a stitch that wraps around the outside of the puff going in and out of the middle. Pull on the thread to give it tension and create the petal shape. Make 6 evenly spaced stitches like this; each one creates a petal.

4. Fill the center of the puff with bead embroidery. Yellow crystals were used in the middle here and

blue seed beads define the center circle. You can also embellish it with more beads and sequins but remember to leave space for the pins!

5. Make the wrist band by cutting a rectangle of fabric, 8" x 4 3/4". Press 3/8" of each long side of the rectangle to the wrong side. Now press a fold down the center of the length with wrong sides together. Try on the wrist band. You want a snug fit plus 2" overlap. Trim off any excess fabric and tuck in the wrong sides at ends.

6. Stitch all the folded edges together using a hem stitch. Sew the snap fasteners on so that they close with a 2" overlap. Embellish the strap with beads and sequins if you wish. Stitch the puff to the middle of the strap.

'be prepared' brooch

I've named this brooch after the Boy Scouts' motto, because it reminds me of the little pencil I wore with my Brownie uniform. Drilling a hole in the end of a pencil stub is a great way to turn an ordinary object into another bead!

MATERIALS

- 2"-long pencil stub
- embroidery floss
- antique brass eyepins and headpins
- about 8 x 3–4mm crystal charms
- 24" of 3/4"-wide ribbon
- 16" of 1/2" polka-dot ribbon
- 2 x brass leaf charms
- seed beads
- 2 x 10mm striped beads or other charms
- 1 1/4" pin back

1. Begin by preparing the pencil to become a charm. Place the end of the pencil in a vice grip and drill a hole about 3/8" from the end. You may need to try this a few times to get it centered, so gather together a bunch of stubs for working with.

2. Poke a pin through the drilled pencil hole to hold the place. Smear some tacky fabric glue around the pencil end. Keeping the pin in place, wrap embroidery thread around the end on both sides of the pencil hole. When you are happy with the look of the embroidery wrap, thread the floss onto a needle and feed the needle through the hole in the pencil.

3. Bring the thread around the pencil and back through the hole in the same direction a few times and then secure the thread by wrapping and knotting.

You can decorate the thread wrap with a few seed beads or a second color of floss if you like.

4. Make the charms by attaching the pencil loop to a beaded eyepin charm. Make two more eyepin charms from the remaining bead, with leaf charms hanging from the eyes.

5. To make the bow, cut a 14" length with straight ends from the 3/4" plain ribbon. Fold the ribbon so that the cut ends meet at the back of the bow. Gather stitch down the center of the bow. Make a double bow form the polka-dot ribbon to fit inside the outer bow.

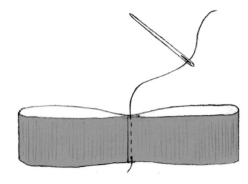

6. Cut a length of ribbon for the ends that is about 6" long. Trim the ends so that they come to an inverted point. Fold the ribbon and tack it in place at the back of the bow so that the ribbon ends look handsome beneath the bow.

7. Fold a scap of ribbon in half lengthwise and wrap it around the center of the stacked bows, hiding stitching and ends. Tack in place. Bring the needle back through the middle of the centerpiece and embellish with seed beads. Bring the needle back through the centerpiece and stitch charms to the bottom of the bow.

8. Complete the bow by sewing the pin back to the wrong side.

TIPS

A hand drill or a small electric drill with a 9/8" bit can be used to make the hole in the pencil but a sharp 3/8" bradawl will do the trick if you have neither. Have some fabric glue and pins on hand for attaching the ribbon to the end of the pencil.

VARIATIONS

Bows can be made with any size of ribbon, but you may need to extend the size to balance wider ribbon. Also consider a patterned ribbon, doubling the bows or using just one end of ribbon for the 'tie.' The small double bow shown left omits the pencil and just uses a delicate bit of chain with crystal charms to make a more elegant statement.

sunset collar

Detachable lace and beaded collars were very popular in the 1930s and 40s. Adding a collar can turn a casual T-shirt into something altogether dressier.

MATERIALS

- 60" x 2½" rectangle of silk fabric for beading and tie
- 60" x 7" rectangle of silk fabric
- 60" x 12" rectangle of chiffon
- nylon thread
- 11° cut seed beads in matching transparent color
- 7mm cupped transparent yellow sequins

1. Tear your silk fabrics into the listed rectangular shapes. We want gently fraying edges so just make small scissor snips at the correct dimension and then gently tear across the fabric.

2. Fold the chiffon down its length so that the fold is 4" from one long edge and 8" from the other.

3. Place the chiffon fold on the edge of the long length of the larger silk rectangle and gather stitch the three layers together. Pull the gathering stitch until it is 20" long. Make a few backstitches to hold the gathers in place and tie off. Distribute the gathers evenly across the collar and press with a warm iron to hold in place.

4. Take the remaining strip of silk and fold it in the middle along the length. Press with a warm iron to create a crease mark in the center. Fold the long raw edges together to meet at the crease mark. Press with a warm iron and then re-press the center fold.

5. Find the center back of the collar and the middle of your folded tie strip and align them. Place the gathered edge of the collar inside the folded strip with the collar edge butted up to the center crease of the tie strip. Baste the tie strip in place by using a long running stitch (this will be removed).

6. Starting at the neck edge, sew a neat running stitch along the folded edges with nylon thread, topping each stitch on the right side with a seed bead. Make sure you catch all the layers in the running stitch. Remove all the basting stitches.

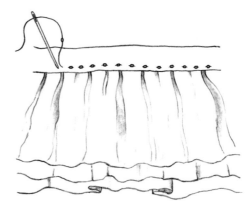

7. Embroider a row of sequins topped with seed beads in the center of the necktie, and a final row of running stitch seed beads at the top. There is no need to hem the tie edges. Press the ties with a warm iron before tying in a bow to wear.

TIP

For an inexpensive source
of silk, look for scarves at
second-hand shops. If they
are pure silk, it is easy to pop
them in a dye bath to get a
range of similar colors.

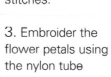
spiky daisy skirt

This was a plain black, linen A-line skirt with a separate border. While embroidering beads all over the skirt would be a daunting task, sticking to the hem or a single motif is easily managed in an evening's sewing session.

MATERIALS
- purchased skirt
- 3 skeins of turquoise green and one of grass-green cotton embroidery floss
- 1 skein each of Rachelette by Caron Colors in A94 (raspberry sorbet), A34 (burgundy red), A154 (golden yellow) and A59 (orange-gold). This is an embroidery nylon tube with a sparkle fill thread. Alternatively, you can use another ribbon embroidery or knitting thread.
- ³/₈ ounce of 11° tricut seed beads in pale green
- ³/₈ ounce of 11° pink seed beads
- ³/₈ ounce of 11° orange seed beads with silver lining
- ³/₈ ounce of 11° amber tricut seed beads
- ³/₈ ounce of 11° dark red tricut seed beads
- enough lining fabric to cover embroidered area. This skirt used about 28" of a cotton quilting fabric. For a winter skirt, which will be worn with tights, I recommend a slippery lining fabric.
- 2 colors of 6mm green sequins
- 4 colors of 10mm sequins for flower centers
- nylon beading thread

1. Lay the skirt flat on a table and draw the flower and leaf motif,

using the illustration as a guide, with chalk pencil. Just draw circles to indicate the flowers and dots for the sequins. If you are unhappy with the placement of the motifs, spray some water on the area. The chalk will disappear and you can iron the skirt dry and start again.

2. When you are happy with the placement of the motifs, clamp on the embroidery hoop and begin embroidering the stem and leaf shapes with the turquoise cotton thread using running and whip stitches (see pages 34 and 36). Use all six plies of the thread for a nice thick line. The whip stitch is done with the same color of turquoise thread as the running stitch but you may like to do the 'whip' in the second color of green thread. Use the second color of green thread to fill in some of the flower leaves with clustered running stitches.

3. Embroider the flower petals using the nylon tube

ribbon. Leave a ³/₄"-diameter circle in the center of the flowers for the beading and sequin. Radiating out from this ³/₄" circle make long stitches, between ¹/₂"–³/₄", with embroidery ribbon. There are about 15 petals on each flower. Make several flowers of each color.

4. Now for some beading! Have your embroidery hoop in place each time you begin a new area and make frequent knots on the wrong side of your work to protect your beading. Thread your beading needle with the nylon thread and begin by filling in the center of the flowers. Use pink, orange, amber or dark red beads to match or contrast with your flower petals. Make beaded loops of 9 beads around the petal edge. You will be able to fit about 10 tightly clustered loops. Knot on the wrong side after each loop. Make an inner circle of another set of 7-bead loops inside the first group of loops. This time you will fit about 6 loops. This will make a densely beaded 3-D flower center. Finally stitch a 10mm sequin and bead in the center of each flower.

5. Stitch single green sequins in the background, using a pale green bead in the center to hold them in place. The green sequins can also be used to indicate berries on the end of the stems. Stitch 4 green beads around the background sequins and 3 along each side of the leaves.

6. To make a pattern for lining the hem of the skirt, lay the skirt on a flat work surface. Pin a piece of tissue smoothly to the area that you want to line, along the hem, side seams and border seam. Mark the pin placement on the tissue and remove from the skirt. Lay the tissue flat and draw smooth lines with a pencil connecting your marked pin dots. Add a ¹/₂" seam allowance and a 1" hem allowance.

7. Cut this pattern piece twice from your lining fabric. Press the ¹/₂" border seam allowance to the wrong side of the lining fabric. Pin the wrong side of the lining, with the pressed border seam allowance folded under, to the wrong side of the skirt. Finger press the side seam allowance in place so that they match at side seams and pin. Finger press the hem allowance in place so that it is ¹/₄" shorter than the skirt hem allowance. Check to make sure no areas of the lining are pulling. Stitch in place using blind stitch. Press and go!

THINGS TO LOOK FOR IN A PURCHASED SKIRT TO EMBROIDER:

- Stable, not stretchy fabric. No knit fabrics, as your embroidery hoop will easily distort the fabric.

- Firm but not too dense a weave. A linen/rayon/cotton blend is perfect because the needle passes easily through the airy weave and it has a nice drape. Beware of tightly woven denims for your first project. They are suitable for embroidery but a looser weave will make your work go faster and more comfortably.

- Opaque fabric: you don't want to see the wrong-side thread loops showing on the right side. Put your hand behind the fabric to determine how opaque it is. Black, red or darker colors are easy to work with.

- My skirt has a separate hem border with a slight flair. Although the skirt was bought unlined it is easy to create a pattern to line this border area. The border seam makes stitching the lining easy and invisible. If there is no border seam you can embellish with a line of purchased ribbon or ric rac to conceal where the lining is added to the hem of the skirt.

- You can also purchase a skirt with a full lining to save yourself time. If the lining is stitched to the hem you will need to unpick this stitching before you begin so that you are only embroidering the skirt fabric, not the lining. The lining can then be tacked back in place after the embroidery is complete.

home decoration

Why not decorate your house, too? Beads look good all over your home – especially in winter, when they can really shine.

bead buttons

These buttons can be used to decorate clothing as well as interior furnishings. Use them to replace existing buttons, or to turn them into brooches just add a pin back (see picture on page 128).

MATERIALS

- 1½"-diameter wood disk blanks (from craft shops) or flat buttons, or size to fit your project
- scraps of fabric, plain or with a small pattern
- embroidery threads
- very tiny seed beads: 15° or small charlottes are particularly effective on this small scale. 3mm crystals and sequins can also be used.
- fiberfill stuffing
- scraps of craft felt or leather for backing
- pin backings (optional)

1. Use a chalk pencil to draw around your button or wood disk onto the fabric. This will be the area that you embroider. Draw a second circle, with a diameter ¾" larger than your button. Later you will cut the fabric along this line to make the button covering.

2. Pop the fabric into a small embroidery hoop. Stitch the embroidery and beads onto the fabric with all the knots on the fabric back. Simple patterns work best on this small scale. The diagram on the right is for a small forget-me-not pattern. The stems are made with whip stitch. The leaves

are small chain stitches and the centers of the flowers are filled with French knots. Each French knot circle is outlined with tiny seed beads and opaque green 3mm crystals form the dots.

3. Cut the fabric out along the outer line. Sew a gathering stitch ⅛" in from the cut edge (as for a yo-yo puff, see page 44). Place a small amount of stuffing on top of the button and then put the fabric on top. How much stuffing used will determine whether the button is flat or very rounded. Experiment until you get a look you like. Pull the gathering stitch tight so that fabric gathers around the button form. Make a few more stitches on the wrong side of the button until the fabric is tightly and evenly gathered. Secure with several backstitches and a small knot. Cut the thread.

4. Cut a circle from the felt that is ¼" smaller than your button diameter. Use fabric glue to attach the felt backing, hiding all the stitching and knots on the back of the button. Either sew this to the item or attach a pin backing.

TIP
If you would like to bead new buttons for a
garment, remove the existing buttons with small
scissors or a seam ripper and use these as your
button form.

bead bouquet

Making flowers from seed beads and wire is referred to as French flower beading. Pop this small posy in a vintage glass perfume bottle and admire it as a boudoir bouquet, or attach a pin back and wear it as a brooch.

MATERIALS
- 4mm pink round cut crystals
- fine Fireline or 10lb test weight fishing line
- 28- or 32-gauge wires in green and pink
- green and lilac seed beads
- 2 x 0mm pearls, one pink, one purple
- 4mm red round cut crystals
- 3mm lilac round cut crystals
- green embroidery floss

1. Begin by weaving the main flower petals out of the pink crystals. Use the Fireline or fishing line to weave the crystals together in the pattern below. This is a variation of the right-angle weave that tapers at the top with decreases. When all the beads have been woven in place, weave the thread ends through the beads until they meet. Tie in a double knot and place a drop of super glue on the knot and trim the ends. Weave 3 petals in this manner.

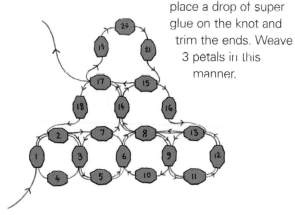

2. Using a 16" length of pink wire, weave it through the perimeter beads for each petal, as in the diagram (near right). Twist the wires together at the bottom. Do this for each of the three petals. Do not trim the wire ends yet.

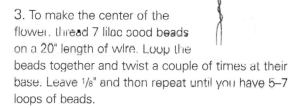

3. To make the center of the flower, thread 7 lilac seed beads on a 20" length of wire. Loop the beads together and twist a couple of times at their base. Leave ⅛" and then repeat until you have 5–7 loops of beads.

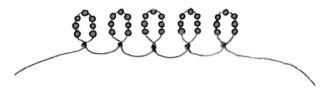

6. The crystal berries are woven with wire in a right-angle weave. Three units of 4 beads are woven. The fourth unit links back in a circle so that in the illustration below, the shaded bead is the first bead. Finally the top 4 beads are woven together in the circular right-angle weave pattern. The wires are woven out the other end, twisted a couple of times and covered in 6–10 seed beads to make a stem. There are 2 lilac crystal berries and 1 red crystal berry.

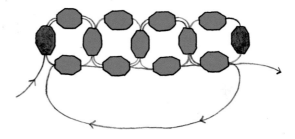

4. Use the green seed beads and 20" lengths of green wire to make 2 stems with 5–7 leaves each, as in the diagram above. Twist the ends together but don't trim them yet.

5. This posy has 5 berries. Two of them are made up with stems covered in 6–9 lilac seed beads, followed by a pearl and then 3 seed beads. Bring the wire back down through the pearl and the stem beads. Twist the wires together but don't trim yet.

7. Assemble the posy by pinching the lilac loops from step 3 together to form the center of the petals. Place the petals around the center. Add the stems of leaves and berries. Arrange them so they are at different heights, gripping all the wire stems together. The wire stem (after the beads) should be about 2¹/₂" long. Fold the bottom of the wires back and trim at different lengths within the stem. Begin winding the green floss around the wire stems starting where the beads end. Wind the thread close together so that it covers all the wire. When you get to the bottom of the wire you may need to fold a little more wire back on itself so that the thread doesn't slip off, or you can use a dab of Tacky fabric glue to hold it in place. Wind the thread back up the stem a little, knot and weave in the end with a needle. Trim the thread ends.

rosy pillow

Combinations of bead and wool (crewel) embroidery are a great way to warm up your home decoration during the winter months. A simple flower design such as this could be applied to curtains, blinds, cushions, or throws.

MATERIALS

- purchased pillow with removable cover
- pink wool yarn (crewel yarn is ideal but scraps of knitting yarn will also work)
- 6° tubular iridescent seed beads in pink and blue
- 11mm flat turquoise sequins

1. Remove the cushion cover and draw the motif onto a corner or center of the cover with a water-soluble fabric pen.

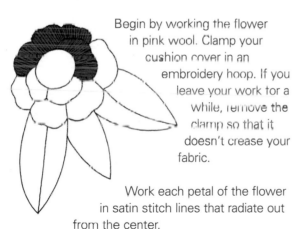

Begin by working the flower in pink wool. Clamp your cushion cover in an embroidery hoop. If you leave your work for a while, remove the clamp so that it doesn't crease your fabric.

Work each petal of the flower in satin stitch lines that radiate out from the center.

2. When you have completed all the wool embroidery, use the pink beads to outline the petals and fill in the center of the flower.

3. Use the blue beads to outline the leaf petals. Couch lines of blue beads to fill the leaves as above.

4. Use the turquoise sequins to fill in the remainder of the leaves.

TIPS

This is a good way to dress up an inexpensive pillow. Look for pillow covers made in heavy fabrics such as velvet, corduroy, or chenille. Alternatively, choose a pillow cover with a pattern and embellish it with beads to make it unique.

silver flower lamp

Lampshades are a great place to add beading: glass beads catch the light and reflect sparkles. Add a seed-bead fringe or crystal tassels to the bottom of a lampshade, or make wire-beaded flowers to sprinkle all over, as here.

MATERIALS
- silver seed beads
- 28-gauge wire
- purple sequins
- purchased lamp and shade

1. Thread 8¹/₄" of seed beads onto the wire. Make 7 x 1¹/₈" bead loops with 2" between each loop (as shown in step 3 for the bead bouquet on page 119).

2. Coil the 7 petals into a flower shape. Thread a sequin onto one end of the wire; weave the sequin into the center of the flower and the wire ends to the back. Twist the wire ends together to hold the flower shape.

3. Poke two holes near each other on the lamp shade where you want each flower to be. Weave one wire end through each hole and then knot or twist the wire ends together on the inside of the shade. Trim the wire ends to ³/₈" with flush cutters.

4. Place flowers all over the lampshade in a random pattern.

TIP
To poke holes in the lampshade to thread the wire ends through, use a bradawl or a tapestry needle.

index

dedication

To Orillia, for your patience, interest, and persistence! One day you will be able to dedicate a book to me.

acknowledgments

Thank you to everyone who helped to make this book so lovely: Jenny Wheatley for her editing and good spirit, Dawn Mason for her advice, Kate Whitaker for her lovely photographs, and Susan for her help.

The models were all charming as well as beautiful: thank you Jenny, Laura, Rosie and Julia. Thanks to the Beaumont-Epstein family for the use of their home, especially to Henny for being there and Fudge for his modeling abilities. (Bubbles would like her modeling acknowledged as well.)

And finally thank you to my family; Orillia, Quinte, and David for their patience, help, understanding, and coffee service while I worked on this book!

resources

Beads come in so many varieties, and fortunately most are available to the home beader through the Internet. Each season new designs are available so keep checking out what's offered.

Most of the basic designs such as 11° seed beads, sequins, findings, and crystals are available at your local bead shop. Support your local shop and buy those where you can actually see and touch them. The Internet is an amazing source for unusual beads and findings. Beads are small so they don't cost much to ship. Below is a list of some of my favorite suppliers, but new ones are constantly appearing, so keep your eyes open.

For vintage and unusual seed beads, I shop at www.empyreanbeads.com

For beads and unusual findings, I look on www.etsy.com

For new and antique ethnic beads, I shop at Happy Mango Beads: www.happymangobeads.com

Search "craft materials" using a search engine. This is a good place to buy beads when you only want a small quantity. Perfect when you are starting out. I found most of my lovely antique brass and copper findings from Lululala land http://www.etsy.com/shop.php?user_id=5120476 on Etsy.

Check out my blog for further listings: www. jujulovespolkadots.typepad.com